OUR ANCESTORS
DID NOT BREATHE THIS AIR

Beltway
EDITIONS

OUR ANCESTORS DID NOT BREATHE THIS AIR

Afeefah Khazi-Syed · Aleena Shabbir · Ayse Guvenilir
Maisha M. Prome · Mariam Dogar · Marwa Abdulhai

Beltway
EDITIONS

Edition, copyright © 2022 Beltway Editions

www.beltwayeditions.com

Printed in the United States of America 10 9 8 7 6 5 4 3 2

Cover Art: Zoe Norvell
Illustrations: Afeefah Khazi-Syed
Photographs: Mariam Dogar, Afeefah Khazi-Syed
Book Design: Jorge Ureta Sandoval
Author Photos: Yusra Aziz, Mariam Dogar, Yousef Mardini, Claire Traweek, Zoha Rizwan, Rumaisa Abdulhai

Acknowledgments

Some of these poems first appeared in The Beltway Poetry Quarterly (www.beltwaypoetry.com) and MIT's American Asian Initiative Zine.

The making of this anthology was supported in part by grants from the Council of Arts at MIT (CAMIT) and MIT MindHandHeart.

ISBN: 9781957372006

Beltway Editions (www.beltwayeditions.com)
4810 Mercury Drive
Rockville, MD, 20853
Indran Amirthanayagam: Publisher
Sara Cahill Marron: Publisher

to our people —
  past and present

TABLE OF CONTENTS

ON BEING REAL

ON THE GROUND BENEATH ME

OUR ANCESTORS DID NOT BREATHE THIS AIR

Afeefah Khazi-Syed · Aleena Shabbir · Ayse Guvenilir
Maisha M. Prome · Mariam Dogar · Marwa Abdulhai

Beltway
EDITIONS

Dear Reader,

Our journey began with a simple challenge among college friends.

One week. One poem. One story to tell.

We met as undergrads at MIT, brought together by the many things we shared: the challenges of being women in STEM, our lifelong pursuits of becoming better Muslims, and the exhaustions of drinking from the academic firehose. Over time, we discovered yet another thing we had in common: a love for poetry. We met up in dorm rooms late on Friday nights, sitting on hand-me-down carpets and taking turns reading aloud poems new and old. We began to gather our work and soon found ourselves with enough poems to create the anthology you now hold in your hands.

So much has happened since then. On the morning of March 10, 2020, we awoke to utter chaos as MIT joined universities across the country in declaring an emergency COVID-19 evacuation. What was expected to last a few weeks has persisted to this day. It has upended our plans, separated us from each other geographically, and taken the lives of loved ones near and far.

The ongoing pandemic is a stark reminder of the fragility of life and inequities that exist globally. With each new variant, the virus disproportionately affects vulnerable communities —medically, socially, and economically. In the midst of it all, we recognize that our anthology stands as a testimony to the privileges we hold. We live within easy access to immediate healthcare. We continued to receive support and resources towards finishing our degrees at MIT during the pandemic. We can already access COVID-19 booster vaccines while so many people around the world, including those in the countries we come from, have yet to receive their first dose. We acknowledge that we have these privileges at the cost of others and therefore it is important for us to be advocating for a just and equitable world.

Our work also took form at the same time as a global reckoning of deep-rooted apartheid, systemic injustice, and longstanding conflict. From the killing of George Floyd, in addition to countless other Black people, to the continued murder of Indigenous peoples. From the unceasing war crimes in Palestine to the ongoing genocide of Uyghurs in China. From the exacerbated crisis in Afghanistan made in part by the US to the continued socio-economic turmoil in Venezuela. This list is by no means complete —we could easily fill the pages of a book much longer than ours.

However, we derive hope and inspiration from the fact that individuals from all walks of life have joined together to fight systemic racism and police brutality in a way we have never seen before. By protesting oppressive forces around the world, supporting the generational work of our Black brothers and sisters, and holding our politicians accountable, we are beginning to see the impact that collective actions can have in demanding change. It is our hope that this widespread alliance prevails and continues to chip away deep-rooted, institutional injustice in the US and beyond.

All of these feelings have taken root in our poetry, finding resonance in the crises, injustices, and hardships our own families, countries, and communities have endured long before and during our lifetimes. Each poem in this anthology is a piece of our generational struggle, of the pain we carry, and of hope.

Another vital motivation behind our poetry is representation. Only in writing poetry together and encountering the works of other poets of color, have we experienced a formerly missing piece in our literature. A piece that converges at the crossroads of who we are: children of immigrants, women, Muslim. A place of rich literary potential still untapped and with so much to give, if only given a chance to be seen and heard.

Through poetry, we want to foster empathy and mutual reciprocity for those who don't often see someone like us within literary spaces. We want to fight against the stereotypes that are often placed upon us in the many intersectional facets we encapsulate. We often find that the few voices that do exist frequently get extrapolated to the experiences of many. As diverse as our voices may appear to be, from South and West Asia to Latin America to the United States to the greater ummah, we are not tokens of our people. This book presents a narrative true to our own lives and experiences that resonates deeply within us.

A lot has changed since we first committed to holding each other accountable to our creative voices. We've graduated from college. We've moved to different cities. We've started graduate studies at institutions across the country. At the time of writing this, we haven't been able to sit together in the same room since 2020, but our Zoom "windows" have kept us together. Between virtual dinners, newly adopted cats, and the offscreen voices of family members, we've grown closer through intimate glimpses into each other's lives. Through it all, the one thing that has stayed constant is this. Our poetry. Our anthology. Our quest to piece together an ode to the places and people we come from.

We often pause to remind ourselves that we are the product of centuries of trailblazing. Each of our ancestors has pushed forward boundaries in their own worlds, in their own ways. We too strive to push the boundary of what is possible, within our lives, within our careers, within our poetry. And we could not do this without the people who have come before us.

The journey of creating an anthology is not easy, but as we reach the end almost three years later, we see that it has given us so much more than we could have ever anticipated. We've crossed paths with friends new and old. We've written on dorm room carpets and at sunlit desks and in Zoom calls spanning thirteen hour time zone differences. We've grown as people and as poets. And we have put together this collection, woven from both the heartstrings of loss and the joy of passed down memories.

Full of gratitude and great hope, we give you our anthology, made with a piece of each of us. Perhaps, dearest reader, you may find a fraction of yourself here, too.

With Love,
The Poets of *Our Ancestors Did Not Breathe This Air*

ON MOTHERS

Parachute

Afeefah Khazi-Syed

every time i settle at your feet
with a bowl of coconut oil in hand
swirled and warmed
for exactly fifteen seconds
in the microwave
i feel generations

the hands of each and every one of them
must have also moved like yours
working through knots of
carelessness and exhaustion

the wrinkles on your fingers
must have been passed down
through hidden battles
i will never know of

and this massage routine
must have grown in perfection
through centuries of
Ammis and Nanis and Dadis

when you neatly fold my hair
into your signature braid
something tells me
these words have been said before

"when will you start taking care of yourself?"
i answer by asking you the same.

A sampling of my favorite lullaby

Ayse Guvenilir

Knowing my fatiha and ABCs
tracing them in a book you drew for me.

Los pollitos dicen

Looking for you through the cafeteria doors
to plant a lipstick kiss on the cheek
I would not wipe away.

Pío pío pío

Scooting my way into the uprooted sidewalk
you helped me limp home.

Cuando tienen hambre

Missing (almost) every half-day saturday
in montbonnot because you let us.

Cuando tienen frío

Struggling with an essay in 4th grade, you said
"write write write and figure out the rest later."

Su mamá le busca el maíz y el trigo

Even with yours needing help limping to the bathroom
you took me to soccer.

Les da la comida y les presta abrigo

Getting me a present
whenever it was someone else's birthday.

Acurrucaditos bajo sus dos alas

Cooking my friends turkey meals
my favorite part the way you made the stuffing
with spinach and strawberries.

Duermen los pollitos

Changing the emphasis from me to yours
and I'm not there to lift your load—

Hasta el otro día

I'm sorry.

I swear you were here

Mariam Dogar

Head on lap
Fingers stroking hair
It's not that I couldn't live without this
It's that I don't want to

**

In your eyes, the fear
The acceptance of the fight
The will for me to be at ease

In my eyes, headlights

**

Wigs. Poison. Mastectomies.
You present the plan
Like you're discussing the menu

**

Coming back to you is
The first sip of water after breaking a fast
I know
I've been away too long

**

If I memorialize a moment before it is over
Are you already gone?

**

Being around you is bittersweet

I want to hold your hand
But I don't want you to see how much this is hurting me
When I'm with you, you never cry
When you think I'm not looking, I see your tears

**

Nothing these hands can do
Seem to have any meaning
Unless they're next to you

**

I keep wondering
Will this be the last?

**

"In the grand scheme of things
It's nothing
I am just dying a little bit faster than the rest of you"

**

It is not nothing

**

It's hard to be weak
When you are strong

It's hard to be strong
When you are weak

**

"Some people are gone in an instant
I get to say goodbye"

**

Why did we never say goodbye?

**

tranquility

Marwa Abdulhai

you waited to pick me up before the bell
bringing leftover snacks from your preschool party
we sat in the parking lot
i ate the last doughnut while
you listened to my day in a language
you did not completely understand

you earned your first paycheck at forty
the hope of a new journey in your eyes
asking me to print pages upon pages of colouring books
for the kids who adored you as much as we

you always know where to find
missing things
the hijab tangled in piles of laundry
keys hidden in clutters of pockets
you told me to say
inna lillahi wa inna ilayhi raji'un
when asking Allah to return that which belonged to Him

you remembered the day of every exam
a bottle of zamzam in your hand
i always wondered how it lasted
till the end of senior year

the alarms always begin at three in the morning
your heart in prayer for the dreams of others
your motivations have never been for this earth
you are a tranquillity

i feel the فرشتے around you, ammi

Our Story

Aleena Shabbir

You were my very first friend
I don't remember a lot
Birth, first steps, nor chubby cheeks
But you saw it all

Your absence gave me the worst panic
I cried rivers in kindergarten
Every morning when you tried to go to work
None of your afternoon promises could sooth
The child who only knew love by you

I looked forward to spending time with you
By your side as you cooked breakfast for two
I yearned for your attention, but you reminded me:
"Tardiness for school signals a bad day"

I made it so far through your endless sacrifices
Feeling the burden of putting you through so much
You always comforted me — my happiness being yours
Eternally exhausted, with eyes that lit up at the sight of me

The first heart I ever broke was yours
Letting you down so badly
It still haunts me to this day
You've always chosen to forgive
Never-ending love and compassion through the pain

I'm so lucky that my first word
Was the most important thing to me

میں آپ سے بہت زیادہ پیار کرتی ہوں

Why I Don't Celebrate Father's Day

Maisha M. Prome

On Father's day,
I made my dad
a Father's day card.

He just looked at it
and said,
"Go give it to your mom."

ON BEGINNINGS

Since the Day I Arrived

Maisha M. Prome

A sunny new day
A paint-splashed sky
A trunk packed full
A four year's supply
A scarf just as blue
Covers my face as I cry
I've mourned the day I would leave
Since the day I arrived

A twin-stacked building
A bright green lawn
A never-ending hallway
A September song
A promise of growth
In the four years to come
When the car pulls away
it leaves me somewhere
I finally belong

Search

Aleena Shabbir

Growing up with a mission on my mind
Tougher than any puzzle
"Everything is so masked; what even is real?"
I've been pondering since that moment

Living in fantasies
Reality is so far
Bias and fabrications, such obstacles
No way to filter them out

So cynical
Complacency takes over
Self-sabotage masked as control
Becoming what I hate most
I stopped trying,

    searching,
    empty, purposeless

Seven years lifeless, unguided wandering
Love for learning and understanding long gone

Watching the world brainwashed, too
Fake news scandals and information choked down
The significance of an unending fight for understanding

Now
Brought back to life
Vowing to never give up on what's important to me
Refreshed and determined
Awaiting tomorrow

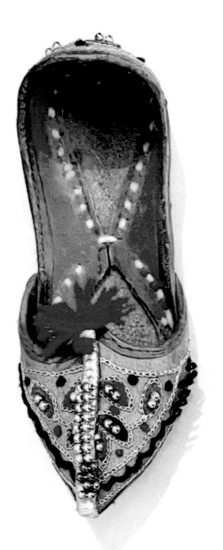

Carving

Mariam Dogar

I am from her

> Nose molded in the crib
> Family names pressed into pores

> Eyes learned to see in the dark
> Kajal outlining every scene

In the mirror, I see her

> Forehead covered at night
> Perfect dupatta-rounded thoughts

> Ears kissed by sweet whispers of Qur'an
> Blessings to all my dreams and fears

Now, I can no longer ask her

> If the sculpting was finished
> before she could never touch again
> If she craved to mold me further
> before her final signature

> Teardrops taught me more than anyone else ever did

> The end of her leaves me
> Questions like fading imprints

How will I do justice to the beginning of ourself
when I must craft the next beginnings
alone?

The Prequel

Afeefah Khazi-Syed

my father was born under kerosene lamps
in a place where monkeys taught children to
spring from the river-blue cement roofs
onto fields of crunchy-green grass

where the laughter of
playing in the streets blended with the
crowing of roosters:
the perfect alarm clock

where kites adorned the sky
glistening in the sunshine and where hot
street-side pakoras were perfect for a rainy day

left behind
for flick switch / mechanical ring / lone star night

journey of a single canvas suitcase

never forgetting to
return to that place
in time, holding the
hands of his own kind

This is Where
The Story of You
Began

ON SUMMER

2009

Aleena Shabbir

9:30 - 11 AM, Art House:

I miss the simplicity of these times
The abundance of laughter
Endless smiles and sunshine
The small shed, filled to the brim
With paint and clay
Tables and kilns scattered
Drinking gallons of juice every morning
As motivation to finish our pottery
Music from the radio numbing our thoughts
The camaraderie, our special glue

11 AM - 12:30 PM, Franklin's Field:

When I smash the dodgeball in your face during All Sports
We always take ourselves far too seriously
And dump coolers of water onto the losing team
Jumping to heights we didn't know existed

1:30 PM - 3:00 PM, Computer Lab:

How about a break from the outdoors?
Something a little more tame
Just
Kidding
Nerdy kids thirsting for a Pulitzer
Writing our own stories and reports
Weekly editions of our own little fun

3:00 PM - 4:30 PM, Room 416:

Always saving the best for last, right?
How could I forget about you?
Surrounded by teenage testosterone
The only girl for three weeks
Building robots that come to life
Soldering friendship through metal and care

August 11, My Heart:

Not a goodbye, but a "see you later"
I never felt yearning like that before
Marking my calendar for next year
Praying for a quick trip around the sun

Side effects of summer may include

Mariam Dogar

Clear bones and good skin
A sentimental road trip playlist
Sunset-induced hypnosis
Always being at your stickiest

Watermelon and mango and pineapple
A mouthful of ocean spray
Sand stuck in the pages of your novel
Poolside overheating at midday

An explosion of freckles
Windswept and wild hair
Cherry-stained lips on vanilla cream cones
Bedtimes chosen without a care

An overabundance of joy
An acceleration of time
The lightest days of the year
Signed by sunburns and tanlines

Do You Wanna Go To Target?

Maisha M. Prome

Do you wanna go to Target?
We have time to spare
And on our way we can discuss
The joys of wiggly air

We have to go see a movie
Because with Disney we're obsessed
Then we can drop by karaoke
Sing until we're both Speechless

Let's go see the fireworks
We'll take the long way home
Past the murals, through the tunnels
Laughter echoing under the Dome

Can't miss those Haymarket deals
Hydrangeas tinged in pastels
Revere Beach, an ocean breeze,
A buffet laid out on shells

Brownies, cheesecakes, macarons
Judge my baking experiments
Spend the evening watching anime
About some high school nonsense

Heatwaves we will weather
By the fifth floor AC
Break our backs moving boxes
Walk to the Port by the Sea

Summer research, unknown futures
Stay up late just because
Laying in a field of grass to find
Jupiter among the stars

August ends so quickly
What a time to be alive
Hold onto this summer with me—
We'll do it all again next time

when i think sunshine

Ayse Guvenilir

flying barefoot, barely being able to catch a breath from all this chasing, laughing, the nights seeming to last forever until they ended and it was a new day and we were fasting. sun blazing, we went outside anyways, playing until we could eat and it would be never-ending night once again. maybe this time, there were no man hunts, but always some sort of game, certainly a feeling of having to pee constant until it was over and back home, my feet were washed of the grass stains left behind and to cool the blazing of the sun. a new day so heavy, it felt like we were the ocean, swimming we were instead of running and i never did get to jump into the pool with my shoes on. it was once, but the rain was burned into the memory of my three-layered skin. every day, something new or old—riding bikes, dodging balls, shooting hoops, exploring forests. running like time did not exist. summer was on fire, even if it was raining, and *we* were invincible until we were no longer nor was it summer—

and Real Life starts up
dreams of never-ending night
when i think sunshine.

ON LOVING

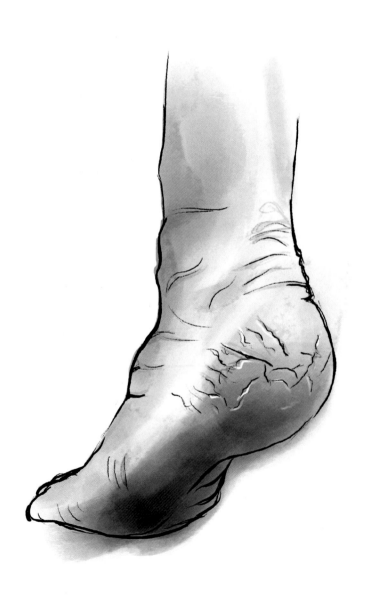

Morning Echoes

Afeefah Khazi-Syed

Bade Dada,

> what did it feel like
> to wake up that morning to echoes of
> **inna lillahi wa inna ilayhi raji'un**
> to realize that after seventy years she
> no longer wakes next to you?
>
> do you forget in the
> split second bliss of the
> few moments you have to yourself
> before you speak
> to a single soul
>
> or is the pain of everything that was and
> everything that you thought there would be
> so unbearable that it takes every
> ounce of life left in your cracked heels
> to move them to the floor
>
> or do you smile
> knowing that God made her for you
> and you for her
> and your souls were meant for
> Jannat-ul-Firdous?
>
> i pray for her
> in the moments that follow after prayer
> but i also pray for you
> and for the faith i heard in your voice
> on that morning of echoes

i don't know how to tell you
i don't love you

Mariam Dogar

every time we speak
i'm reminded of my mistakes
i ignore the heartbeat sirens
the threads of myself screaming
that i owe you nothing

if i told you my words were out of pity or guilt
it would unravel you

so i tape down my teeth
sew shut my lungs
these syllables sit
heavy in my organs
sharp like stones

    i don't know why
    this truth always feels like fire

    i don't know why
    i still want to please you

    i wonder what
    it will feel like on my breath

unused and unnatural
to say those words one day

~~you hurt me~~
i love you
    i wonder if
    i could mean them

if they could ever slip between my lips
like they fall from everybody else's

When in Dialogue

Marwa Abdulhai

A Mormon, a Muslim, and a Hindu sat at the corners
// of a rounded table

Chatting away on the weather and business of the day
They had gathered to discuss Truth
As their souls watched behind happy eyes
Afraid to speak on their creation and existence

They spoke of intentions before conversation
Gathering questions they sought to understand
They were equal partners in search for a reason
For surely, if God willed, God would make
// them one community

The Mormon spoke of her mission abroad
Peace found in disconnecting from the world
The Muslim felt a sense of holy envy
He wished he was more vocal about his faith

The Muslim shared stories of perseverance
// of the last Prophet
Raising the importance of giving to zakat in his faith
He finally felt comfortable stepping away for zuhr salah
The Hindu admitted she could be spending
// more time in prayer

The Hindu believed in many chances at life
She held respect for her parents above all else
Yet confessed she wasn't always so sure of certain traditions
The Mormon expressed she empathized, though she couldn't
// always voice it

The Mormon, the Muslim, and the Hindu
Discussed ideas and not people
In mutual understanding of their differences
Leaving with what was learned and not spoken

A Mosaic

Maisha M. Prome

Like my memories of this country before I left
Melded with the memories I made after I came back
Like the tiled floor after I've slipped and fallen
The patterns stained on my scarf by careful, steady hands
The round yellow dal speckled amongst the long thin basmati
The aromas when you enter the bazaar
Harmoniously clashing, in sync, distinct
Like the essays I write for my humanities classes
An eclectic collection of half-formed ideas
Somehow ground, strung, compacted into coherence
Like the night sky strewn with clouds, simmered in shadow
The needled imprint of the masjid carpet on my skin
The hexagonal cells under the microscope
Packed together in a plant slice
Like remembering my dreams and watching them disintegrate
Every single dawn

"Aleena" isn't what I go by

Aleena Shabbir

It's "jaanu"
when you ask about my day and wish me goodnight

It's "pyaari"
when you kindly request my help or want to talk

Or "pagal"
when you laugh at all my antics and jokes

Sometimes "chalaak"
when I do something that slips your eye

"Meri zindagi"
when we encourage and uplift each other

"Mera dil"
when you're comforting me through pain

It's "behta"
when you announce breakfast

"Larki"
when I sass you

And endless more

Forgive me

When I pause

"Aleena"

I haven't heard that very often

ON THE UNSPOKEN

•

Mariam Dogar

You woke to a surprise on your bed
Pure white sheets stained rusted red

They said it was normal. Nothing to fear
But the sight of your blood kept feeding the tears

You cried for what you couldn't know, but felt
You grieved the innocence that you'd once held

You lost a childhood of skirts and shorts
They now controlled your body parts

The next month, your world turned crimson again
Coach said: "Wear tampons like other women."

At home, you googled what "tampon" means
Then you closed the laptop and quit swim team

Your accidents were public, with family and strangers
You'll never forget *Their* whispers and fingers

You prayed for the pain the others talked about
So that next time, you could catch yourself before spilling out

One month, you're ambushed by two visits
You then leave the masjid entirely to avoid the critics

Sometimes, your brother would throw a fit
He's mad when you aren't praying and he is

It would be simple to explain to him why
But the thought makes you feel small. Instead, you hide

At school, you learn about the menstrual cycle
You hear *Them* in the back: "Periods make girls go psycho."

As the days pass, *They* always have more to say
About what you wear and how you pray

Who you should touch and for how long
Where you should travel and why you're not strong

To you, I say: a woman is not a sin
You're a miracle, sister. You've always been

You bleed and heal as you sprint through life
Your sole purpose, I promise, is not to be a good wife

You carry *Them* in your belly and upon your tongue
Heavy on your shoulders and deep inside your lungs

You are unscripted power, my dear
And We won't forget it

Hold Back

Ayse Guvenilir

"Step up to the line if you were ever judged for the way you speak"

And when she steps forward, you understand it was because she learned English after her mother tongue—after she was 11 years old. A moment, and she, along with everyone else, steps back.

                     "I was never allowed to be myself."

But then

                     "Never allowed to say 'insha'Allah'"

given the chance to share

                     "in public, could never stop"

her throat starts to close

                     "in the middle of my day"

breath catching on each inhale

                     "to put my head down"

and you know the shine in her eyes

                     "and just pray."

isn't from the laughter

                     "Eid-al-Adha sacrifices"

that usually spills easily

                     "had to be made"

from her lips.

                     "in utmost secret."

Though it isn't about you, you can't help but shudder. Your preconceived notions of her innocent Bosnian life shattered. You know your sister in Islam has suffered and now, all you pray for in salah and du'a is a world in which when she's asked to think about the statement to step up to—she doesn't.

i ask for Justice

Marwa Abdulhai

could justice be served to Sacrifice?
she lived in the shadows of her fairer sister
a society where sons were given last names
and daughters were not
they did not belong to their families
she spent years in care of her frail grandparents
soon moving to a strange land with a strange man
dreams of learning The Word only realized
twenty-five years later.

could justice be served to Curiosity?
the lands of Meenambur did not satisfy her thirst
she swallowed whole all they taught her
with her sharp memory and sweeping talents
she swam in the wells at day and cooked at night
trained by her mother for the end of childhood
in marriage at the age of fifteen to a much older man
she gave away all she had to his unsuccessful business plans
with the rest of her life in want of things
that could never satisfy her.

could justice be served to Ambition?
years toiled in hope of an engineering degree
which she did achieve, all and more—
having four children, one after the other
but a family who did not permit her to earn her own.

could justice be served to Hope?
The Word turned against its true meaning
staying at home as her father, brothers, and uncles

prayed at the masjid every Friday
engaging in lengthy debates and conversation
there was no place for her.

i stand in watch of women there and women here
                                       and myself
i see stolen rights
i count moments on these scales
practices mistaken for religion silences our voices
we are blind to the life we all deserved.

My Two Characters

Afeefah Khazi-Syed

somewhere

a boy, four-feet tall
dragging water-filled pots
through a rugged mile
home

a girl, hair twisted
in strips of bright red ribbon
jumping out of a moving rickshaw
an act of defiance
a refusal of going to that place
where children learn to grow

                                        here

                    a man, antique mustached
                         fighting through
                forty miles of rush hour traffic
                        away from home

                    a woman, hair pulled back
                        into a hurried bun
                jumping into the front of her odyssey
                        an act of selflessness
                an assertion of going to that place
                    where children learn to grow

            all hidden in the pieces they sacrifice
                    for two new characters
                who don't know these stories at all

Welcome Home

Maisha M. Prome

August. 36 hours of flying, and I've finally landed in Boston.
The TSA agent finishes checking my bags and hands them
back. Just as I am about to step into the final stretch of
hallway between me and freedom, his voice stops me.
"Miss,"
I turn. "Yes?"
He nods.
"Welcome home."

.

Welcome home.

I have never heard that before.
Not even when I land in my jonmobhumi,
the place I was born
Where the immigration officers glance at my passport
and wave me through the gate
Where the dusty Dhaka air whispers hello
and the humidity wraps me in a hug
The smiles on my parents' faces when they pull up in the car
The sweetness of the mango milk my mother hands
me to last the drive home
My siblings' bubbling voices when I step through the door
All these things whisper, affirm, assure
The words I've never needed to hear aloud.

.

Welcome home.

Words I've never heard once in my life
For the countless times I've stepped out of planes into
Boston Logan or JFK
Where the dry air of the air conditioning hums to
the beat of my heart
As the blue-uniformed officer frowns at my passport
Trying to match it to my hijab framed face
In his eyes I see the cold steel silent distrust
While I try to hide the agony in mine

"You've been selected for a random security check."
Of course.
"Walk through the scanner again."
Ice in their voices. Alarms, handcuffs, gunshots just a button
press away.
"Did you pack these bags yourself?"
They comb through my things. The clock is silent, but I hear
the secondhand tick away.
They never find anything of issue, yet the guilt is always mine
to carry, zipped away into the spaces between my carefully
folded clothes.
Breath held, I rush through the last checkpoints
And exhale only when I'm out the door en route
to the safety of my college dorm

But today,
I am stopped by two words.

"Welcome home."

.

For a minute I am lost
Stilled by the crash of a wave that breaks into small ripples
on sand
Stuttering I thank him, in my head I am dazed
And a few minutes later, as the car races over the highway,
I am surprised to find a tear run down my face.

.

Welcome home.

This should not mean anything.
Home is home whether you're welcomed or not,
As the States has always been for me
It shouldn't make a difference, and yet it does.

Maybe it's because I've spent years always on guard
Holding on my tongue the comebacks to the
"Go back to your country" they will shout at me
Like they've shouted at my parents

And how I've spent years on long haul flights, lying awake all
15 hours thinking
About everything that could/might/will go wrong
When Uyghurs disappear and Guantanamo Bay pricks the
back of my eyelids between wisps of clouds Rohingyas fleeing
houses burned to the ground and smoke is still awash over
Palestinian blood.

It is never the turbulence that agitates my stomach

.

Welcome home

I have only known a world where I am not welcome

.

So when I hear this
From a blue-eyed blonde-haired TSA officer
I find myself at a loss

Sometimes
Acknowledgement can hit like a ton of bricks

Two thoughtful words can sink in
And replay themselves
Every time I see the Boston skyline reflected in the Charles
River on the car ride back from the airport.

ON MIGRATION

a citizenship

Marwa Abdulhai

you step outside when a gush of spice hits the air and you
and your nose
it's embedded deep within the fabrics of your jacket
the tide detergent never seems to mask the smells of
// homeland you are so ashamed of
they ask you why you smell like spice
and why your food has so much pepper

but Vasco De Gama didn't go to India to get pepper

he went to get the haldi in sambaar and chicken jalfrezi
and the zeera in the butter chicken you have when you think
// you've experienced India
you shrug in response
abba told you that you are now an "american"

i remember the time i became a citizen of this country
age 10 two-piece hijab removed for a passport photo
shame knowing you didn't fight for your right to dignity
shame knowing your mother and sisters did the same

you knew it in that moment when you in your two-piece scarf
ran through the aisles of Costco
with your mother in her shiny and new black abaya they stared

and now
you speak in the language of your colonizers from 1858

it would only be years later
when you were gifted the power of the pen
to acknowledge
the seams in the fabrics of your jacket

the middle between us

Ayse Guvenilir

they left early
before the morning

we're boarded

& we don't hear from
them again until the
unreliable wifi lets them
connect back to us

waiting for the shuttle

waiting to go outside

oh wait

we can't. it's not safe

waiting for tomorrow
& our parents sleep.

except they wake every hour
waiting for this day
years in the making.
the unfortunate reality
that a death had to be
the bridge to this—
waiting.

on the other side she
smiles scared of leaving.
scared of never coming back
"estoy visitando" she'll say but
we all know that
was never the plan.

scared of this day she
knew was coming but
postponed for her own
reasons after the
bureaucracies finally
stopped delaying passports
& widows' pensions.
scared because
this was home.

where her hijos no
longer in this country were
raised. where her first nieta
her mamá & most recently
her esposo were buried.

scared.
& she boards the plane.

when they see her
arriving in a wheelchair
a little smaller than they remember
they smile. she smiles.
& cross the ocean
together.

Serenity. Andhra Pradesh, India. 2019.

A Statement For The Confused

Afeefah Khazi-Syed

my heritage
is a crystal snow globe
meticulously arranged and carefully curated

Hum Saath Saath Hain and warm bowls of haleem alike
surrounded by endless fields of mango trees
framed by the piercing of a macaque-filled mountain
that gives way to intricately adorned lorries
and fresh street-side nariyals

collections of pashminas and chiffons wrapped around
a face whose forehead bows to the ground in namaaz
in remembrance of God being one
captured in between two palms
raised towards the sky

my heritage
is a corningware bowl
always threatening breakage

you see this is who i am
pieces of wannabe snow
orbiting around the very things
that make me who i am

and yet i am forced to grasp onto it all so tightly
    out of fear that someone will come by
        yanking street-side nariyals from collections of pashmina
            claiming that the two should have separated
a long time ago

when my Nana was eight
and his father knew
better than a thousand educated men
"yeh log bhi hamare log hai"

my heritage
is a tattered journal
burned with the hues of a 1947 partition

its contents
abridged and compartmentalized
by colonizers' tales of religious difference
i exist in between the consequences

i have forgotten what it feels like
to walk into a room of people whose ancestors
come from the same land as mine
and not have to explain myself

i have forgotten what it feels like
to raise my hands in group prayer
at the local masjid and hear the name of
my motherland alongside the rest

i have forgotten all but this

my heritage
is all of this
and i simply am

Indian.
Muslim.
Indian. Muslim.
Indian Muslim.

22 Years

Maisha M. Prome

0. Born, without my own consent, and I'm a little mad.

1. Finally on speaking terms with Mom and Dad.

2. Learn to walk, then run, and I run fast

3. Hold my sister in my arms before we step aboard,

4. Home together at last

5. Hold my brother in my arms

6. We grow so fast

7. First grade giggles

8. Second grade laughs

9. Teachers whose love I carry forever in my backpack

10. Playground adventures unsurpassed

11. A decision. A move. A long flight back.

12. *Breathe. Be calm. Adjust. Adapt.*

13. Steady now, it's all moving so fast—

14. Until...suddenly it's...not moving at all, just

15. For a few seconds stalled on a camera centered wall

16. Then I'm running. Through an exam season that will determine everything

17. I run and I run and find myself on an international stage

18. An acceptance letter arrives,

19. Life forever changed.

20. Here I'm running again but faster. And I've never been happier

21. But growing breathless by the hour, it gets harder, how much longer...will I last?

22. I blink and the finish line ribbon slides between my fingers.

It's all gone by so terribly fast.

ON HOME

The sun we haven't felt in years

Mariam Dogar

is seeping through the cracks
of our 3bedroom2.5bathrental.

   My father sees me lying on the sofa feeling.
   \ My father sees me lying on the sofa and asks me
     how I'm feeling.

I tell him about the plant I just placed on the windowsill
and hope will grow here.

Insha'Allah, he speaks to me,
like he spoke to the oranges he grew in Aravwala
as the sun warmed the lands his father fled to from India.

He talks about fresh mangoes for breakfast
and sugarcane cavities by lunch,
40 acres of hard-earned years under the sky,
and his pet monkey that they found roadwise

while we now sit in the squares
of our 3bedroom2.5bathrental.

   All day he's been talking.
   \ All day he's been on the phone talking

A litany of conference calls, project deadlines, KPIs,
and I can't recall the last time he's been outside
of this 3bedroom2.5bathrental,

where he can only converse with his kids in
a language he did not grow up speaking.

But either way, they're always in the basement,
playing games online where they build farms in bytes,
grow crops in clicks, and spend their minutes
never talking to him about Aravwala.

So much space
in a 3bedroom2.5bathrental.

   I can sit on my bed for hours.
   \ I can sit on my bed four hours speaking into my laptop,

talking to economics professors about solving problems,
talking about Arifwala, about Pakistan,
the home he knows, but we do not.

He's just a hallway away,
but I'm the only one the class will listen to
inside this 3bedroom2.5bathrental.

Our home.
One of the many
that live in our heads.

He has a home
that will never live in mine.

   But we are together.
   \ We are together and the sun is peeping through
   the windows.

The fields at sunrise. Arifwala, Pakistan. 2019.

A house isn't a home, but it used to be

Ayse Guvenilir

i once had a foundation
put in place by the choices made when i was a peach seed
that my youngest brother pointed to be grown in the backyard
where i was a monkey swinging
from handlebar to handlebar
where the tangerines finally bloomed subsequently
the vines tethering   me to him   to   him to him
were cut at the middle to and we were in pairs
breaking apart each second we had our house
where they stayed and we left with part of our foundation

the other pair left where the bananas never sprouted
where the peaches no longer grew
though lemons dropping gave hope on burning days
tangerines showered the concrete yard and
eventually they both stopped growing too

Alive

Maisha M. Prome

Rain drums, thrums on the rooftop
To a beat that overtakes the one that keeps me alive
And then slowly sings me to sleep at my desk

Tomorrow maybe, I'll finally get up from this desk
Still can't go outside but we can go to the rooftop
To look at the sky and remember that it's good to be alive

All those years when the city was alive
And yet we sat still and studied, glued to the desk
Only the rain knows reason as it rinses the rooftop

Love Will Keep Us Safe

Aleena Shabbir

Not so tangible
Just a state of mind
A fireplace burning indoors
Second place to a warm embrace of a loved one

When I leave
It's not the place I miss
But the little homes I've built in these bonds
The hugs, warmth, laughter we collected

Through the years
All these homes use so much space
Not on the ground
But the timeshares in my head
Completely owned by mortal angels

I have a hard time adjusting
When I'm somewhere new
Settling down is infinitely scarier
When you don't know what that looks like
Or who will welcome you

Found

Afeefah Khazi-Syed

The thumping of   a
broom from down   below
demanding   a   break from
never ending games   of leapfrog and jump
rope. That night when I sat in the middle of an
empty living room afraid of change much too soon. The
pillow forts and the trains of stuffed animals. The marks of sunken
grass left behind by kiddie pools and slip-n-slides. The evenings spent singing
along to ghazals burnt onto floppy discs. The car horns and hurry of the
streets in Kamalapuram and Banaganapalle and Hyderabad and Chittoor.
With the kids who climbed over fences to play in the snow. All of the mi
casa su casas. Playdates that end with ice cream. Dawats that end with
acidity. In the cups of RoohAfza and bowls of kajur that get passed around
the room. The way my soul feels when my forehead touches the ground
below. Between the chocolate covered almonds. In the twenty people that
sit on top of each other at a table meant for six to eat dining hall food.
Behind unlocked doors and laughs that carry down the hallway and into
late night escapades. In the hidden corners of Stata where the passing of
people carries through day.   The bowl of dal chawal
and shammi kabab served   fresh off the stove when
the sofas are full again. In   the silent suburban nights
and the city lull. And in the   salaams of morning sun.

I have found in so many places
I was found in so many places

I have found so much
in all of these places

ON HOME AGAIN

Dear My Favorite Memories

Ayse Guvenilir

Jumping onto the car roof because you are not walking home in the cold from this restaurant where i only had goldfish and for some reason it's a problem that i (supposedly) never finish my food in fact it's funny too you say i care about your day and i do and i'm touched that it touches you see me from across the room and you scoot your way over and i haven't a clue about this lab report but we put our sweaters on backwards so at least we're warming up this room with book clubs and 320 struggles that you got me through the night when i just wanted this presentation prep to end I'M SINGING down the hallways where you find me, always.

The warmth you feel radiating from me really comes from all of you don't you see formulation and catalyzation that night across the Charles you talked about building while flying i didn't know you appreciated the first time we met i thought you thought i was annoying essays written while making arepas you kept me company.

Reminiscing memories do mean so much to me i don't know how to process so you put on headphones over your earbuds as you backed out the room i'm laughing at the singular mango party of four isn't it obvious that i too am Muslim like you see me as a mentor i'm just lucky getting to

love,
all of you.

March, 2020

Maisha M. Prome

It feels strange to be home
This time of year
The way the sunlight,
    a mix of blazing cream and molten sepia
Filters through the balcony
Dapples through the glass of the coffee table
And sets a silent fire in the teak armrests
The way the tiled floor holds a lingering coolness
    against the soles of my bare feet
The way the ceiling fan is turned all the way down
      revolving lazily like a daydream
The way a certain stillness pervades the furniture,
        the houseplants, the dust that shimmers in the air
Quiet as the winter hands itself over to the coming heat
I have not seen that in a long time
I am usually not home
This time of year

the final destination

Marwa Abdulhai

will i feel my soul
as we ascend to Al-Hayy?
will it be like when our messenger travelled
on the back of Al-Buraq?

if you find yourself in that place
and you don't see me around
ask about me
even if i had smiled upon you
for only a moment

we can meet along the river of our Prophet
i can add your wish list to mine
maybe the birds could give us a ride
to see the sunrise at Al-Aqsa

The Landing

Aleena Shabbir

Each time the plane descends
I can feel the air lift my mother's face
And widen my father's smile
Peace shining in their eyes

Free rides in Joyland instead of Playland
Fried Chicks, not KFC
Filling both heart and stomach
With calories that last a lifetime

The airport, crowded
The crowd, lively
The yelling of different travelers
All coming home

My mamu always there to pick us up
Holding cold, fresh Shezans
A sweetness that can only be tasted
Back in Pakistan

Dear Kashmir

Afeefah Khazi-Syed

you and i, we are not that different
the color of our skin traverses across
the same paint palette at Home Depot
october sky to dark camel
and every shade that falls in between

you wake up to the warmth of sunshine
i wake up to the warmth of sunshine
but yours fights through the Kunlun Mountains
and mine through the Boston Skyline

we both know the smell
of the air just before it's about to snow
but you know other smells too
of sweaty crowds
    chanting in the streets
of mortal shells
    dissolving into thin air
of flesh
     losing its meaning beyond this nationless land

in the moments before i go to sleep at night
the breeze of my ceiling fan reminds me of my
andhra grandmother
and the coolness of her morning terrace

somewhere in the middle of the night
it hits me that i have such fond memories
of a place that takes away yours

it leaves me with nightmares of
patterns of electric fences striped borders
so held up on the You and I that they forget
azadi is what keeps Us alive

i am suspended in the paradox of my homeland

the sun sends to you its warmth
from 92.96 million miles away
we have forgotten how to do the same
from a stone's throw away

ON FAITH

Sixth Grade

Afeefah Khazi-Syed

i started sixth grade hijabi

chipmunk cheeks
framed with a white chiffon
inspiring all kinds of creative ask aways
   no, i do not take a shower in this
   no, the bun in the back is not an alien antenna
   yes, i do have hair,
      in fact a whole head of thick, dark hair

      Sirens blare in the near distance as the air fills with smoke.

i answered all kinds of questions
in sixth grade

where did i find this
unwavering belief and confidence in my deen?

where did i find the stamina
to be okay with singularly defending an entire faith
in sixth grade?

and why did it all come much more easily
back in sixth grade?

      Children's playground burns to the ground at the local masjid.

i notice the incriminating looks
more now
taken left to right up and down

find myself fatigued from the elongated
routine of flying home
feel the stickiness of my looks
when i encompass a new space

you areOff beat

A prosecution of post 9/11 attack against Muslim Americans begins.

there are days when it feels like my imaan
is hanging on by a single thread
and there are days when the connection to God
is felt so deeply into my bones
that tears fall down
to the ground
in sajdah

A year passes before the man is sentenced for a hate crime.

i have even more work to do than
a work in progress

and so again and again
i find myself folding my palms
in the exact same way my
grandmother taught me to
praying for the belief and confidence and strength
i found
in sixth grade

Empty

Ayse Guvenilir

i need to pray after this

it's been awhile and it makes me feel
like there's something missing from inside my chest
like breaths i breathe are borrowed
like exhaling into Allahu'akbar
might seal these holes

Fleeting Faith

Aleena Shabbir

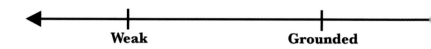

An important part of me
But not everything
My energy was termed "fiery" and "scandalous"
Guilty for being me while loving You

Khutbahs, Jumu'ah, Halaqahs
Rebuilding my safe zones
Reinforcing the solo sincerity
Muslim at my core and foundation

Attacks on my "inability to let you in"
My biggest heartbreak
Shamed for "weak faith"
Struggling through depression

No longer feeling strength
But hoping to return to it
After all if two really love each other
They'll always find their way back

Strong

In love from the first moment
Stabilized and grounded
Discipline and order
Truths I never knew I needed

Islamic School and summer camp
Opportunities to know You more
Falling deeper by the encounter
Seeing the peace You bring others

Clinging on through thick and thin
Eighteen years of trials and bumps
Sticking by Your side
I knew You were worth it

Submission

Marwa Abdulhai

is there such a thing as free will
when our will is the consequence of the opinion
of friends, family, peers
the choices we make are influenced by
the norms and whims of society
we race against time hoping
                    waiting
                            praying for acknowledgment
of any and every kind

i strive to break free of these shackles
i am in Submission of another Kind
to the one and only God—Allah
who created me, for a reason i do not yet understand
Al-Waliyy, Al-Hameed
The Protecting Friend, The Praise Worthy

we ask why there is suffering on this earth
why there is a struggle
if the God we know is All-Merciful and Just
but His Justice is beyond the standards of this world
unveiled to humankind on judgment day
Al-Fattah, Al-Alim
The Judge, The All-Knowing

things may not go according to plan
but everything happens for a Reason
a design of His creation, making
As-Samee', Al-Baseer
The All-Hearing, The All-Seeing

i write my burdens and troubles on this paper
i give this file to You, my Lord
and i leave it up to You
Al-Hakeem, Al-Wadood
The Wise, The Loving

when i come walking to Him
he comes running
when i come crying to Him
he comes smiling
Al-Hayy, Al-Qayoom
The Ever-Living, The Sustainer

Dadi

Mariam Dogar

I haven't seen you in a while,
but today I was told you prayed for me.

And I prayed for the olive oil
when it slipped
   from your hands
      onto my scalp,
aching strands of hair
in the drought of being without you.

I prayed for the way that you warmed your potion
before using it,
the slow swirls of the honey
and the quick whisks of the eggs.

I prayed for your wrinkled palms
and their decades of hidden work;
a thousand back scratches and mango slices and
tummy-ache sodas,
a hundred du'as fanned into the pores of my skin.

For every sugar molecule in a spoonful of halwa,
your two golden bangles that rest on my wrists,
hours of Qur'an we read cross-legged together,
the Insha'Allahs and the Masha'Allahs,
the ways you showed me to always turn to Allah.

For the biggest blessing you ever sent me,
from faith, a leap

                    from halfway across the world
telling my father you accepted that woman—my mother
born in a strange place called New Hampshire.

For all the flavors of sustenance you showed me,
I pray you glow in paradise.

ON TONGUES

Rice

Maisha M. Prome

I was taught this language by my father who
tended these fields as did his parents before him, taught
that this backbreaking labor day after day
is what feeds a newly born country through war and
genocide (that Pakistan wrought). Perfect long white grains
fall into a bowl, glistening multitudes like the
multiplication tables my mother made me memorize at six
Just like my parents did as did their parents before them.
Because with the grain that gave my ancestors sustenance
through the famine (that the British caused), came
the need for careful calculations of impartial portions
and so embedded within the genes they passed down to me
is a binding obligation that I never fail a math test.
Rice, painstakingly multiplied and cautiously divided,
is what has kept us alive.

زبان

مروہ عبد الحی

میری زبان
عجیب سا لگتا ہے نا ؟
میرے منہ سے
لوگ کہتے ہیں کہ میں عرب ہوں
لیکن وہ بارش کے گلیاں
تازہ بنی ایڈلی کی خوشبو
چمکتا ہوا سمندر
میری روح میں چل رہا ہے

zubaan

Marwa Abdulhai

پڑوسیوں کے درمیان بہت سی زبانیں بولی جاتی ہیں
تمل ، کناڈا ، تلگو ، اور اردو
پانچ وقف کے نماز سنائی دیتی ہے
ہم بہت رنگوں سے بنے ہیں

لیکن آپ کو کیسے پتا ہو گا
جب لوگ تو ہمارے دیش کو
ہندوستان بنانا چاہتے ہیں

my language

does it not sound strange

coming from my mouth?

people say that i am arab

but the streets of rain

aroma of freshly made idli

glow of the sea

flow through my soul

اللہ نے ہمیں الگ قوموں اور قبیلوں سے بنایا
تاکہ ہم ایک دوسرے کو جان سکیں
کوئی مجھے بتاو
ہمارے دیش کا سکون کہا گیا؟

there are many languages spoken amongst neighbors

tamil, kannada, telugu, urdu

5 times of salah are heard

we are made of many colours

but how would you know?

when people would like to make this land

just for the hindus

Allah created us of different nations and tribes

so that we may know one another

can someone tell me

where the peace of our nation has gone?

Dots

Aleena Shabbir

Scattered all over my face and neck
Inflammation and pain
White bumps and black blips

Doctors' visits
"Stronger treatment"
"Hormonal changes"

Whispered remarks
"Bumper truck face"
"Pimply queen"
Feeling like they were right

Kneeling, each night, in front of the mirror
Wondering why no one else knew this pain

Nine years later
I finally found peace
The culprit:
Dairy

comb through from root to end

Ayşe Güvenilir

"you look hispanic with those hoops"

"you look *so* turkish"
"you clearly got your saç from here too"

(but you have your mommy's rizos)

the way they say you don't know the dil
the scrunch of their eyes
you hide behind your **madre** for words she could never have taught

unable to detangle adorations your abuelos loved you with
you avoid going near the teléfono when they're on

you take dersler on saturdays
conditioning kelime by kelime that you thereafter forget

you decide to choose the lengua over french
that could brush you closer
to **anlayış** more than maybe a palabra here or there

your hair goes from
düz   to   rizado
and somehow that changes where you're from

---

you give up on trying to make it perfect
on trying to weave each strand seamlessly into the next

you can't braid layered hair without the fringes sticking out

at least, i have never been able to

ON FORGETTING

our kismaat

Marwa Abdulhai

she walks towards the car
the palm of her hand hitting the glass
the other gripping tightly onto her brother
his right hand outstretched towards us
they tell us to ignore her and him
there are so many others
we can't know them all

on the way to dinner we see
his weary feet and frail fingers
peeking out of the black plastic
he remains invisible on these streets
awake all night in the work of his family

25,000 died from hunger yesterday
552,830 are homeless in this land of the free
they say if we work hard enough
we will succeed
anyone can be a millionaire!
but have they forgotten?
we are of Allah's choice

a choice made at the beginning of time
her without a meal and him without a house
and us
with all of the above
perhaps kismaat has it that this is our test

Something, Anything

Maisha M. Prome

I grasp for a moment, a minute, a memory
But I don't even remember your face
All I have is a letter, written two decades ago
That my mother carefully saved
So that one day, I might read it for myself

I couldn't really read at three,
But you, at five, were just old enough to write
And in your looping, stumbling, newborn alphabet
You had laboriously crafted three sentences
Framed in Hello Kitty stickers and doused with spelling mistakes
A kindergartener's first homework assignment
A little girl's first letter
A heartfelt message

> *Prome stay wel.*
> *I haf to go to skool.*
> *I feel ing very sad.*
> *—Noushin*

When my mother first read it aloud to me
I'm sure I missed you too.
Now I hold this letter wishing
I could remember something, anything

Wishing I could at least remember your face.

i remember

Ayse Guvenilir

playing outside
in front of my house
for hours
and not worrying about grown-up things.

tickle fights that made me
laugh so hard my stomach hurt and
i kind of had to poop.

dancing with my brothers
to the best music i'd ever heard
in our family room past my bedtime
on a thursday night.

trying to keep mom upstairs
so she wouldn't know
we were making peanut butter cookies
for her anniversary
while dad was buying flowers.

the longest car rides ever
on our way to south padre island—
my favorite place in the world.

                                         it was a long time ago.

sleeping on a couch with no couch pillows because
our stuff was already gone.

fidgeting my leg because it wouldn't move until
i finally woke up
and saw a white-haired smiling man.

who was he?
why was he holding my foot?

                                        i was annoyed.

realizing my father must be back from miami
back from picking up
two very important people.

thinking
this must be Abuelo—
        my Abuelo—
finally.

                                i felt bad for being annoyed.

and i remember the first time i remember ever seeing Abuelo.

i remember

                                it was a long time ago.

the sound of "hola guapa"
coming from mom's lips
the look on her face when i turned
saw her sitting at the airport cafe.

                                it had been 2 months.

the cries i didn't hear
the stress i didn't feel
the fear i didn't taste.

not being in venezuela
where little bad things here
are huge bad things *there*

not going from hospital to hospital
trying to find just one
that takes Abuelo's insurance.

not hearing the tic of the clock in the background
begging for Dios le bendiga y le proteja
until he could reach help.

not knowing
about Abuelo's stroke
until i saw mom
sitting at the airport cafe.

the emptiness in her world
the shaking in her bones
the restlessness in her eyes.

the guilt in my heart
of not being *there*
of not knowing.

the relief that at least—
            at least—
he's recovering.

and i remember
the promise he made to me—
he's going to live until he's one hundred and fifty.

insha'Allah
he's going to be alright.

he has to.

Oud

Mariam Dogar

In the drawer by my bed
I keep the scent you wore to Eid prayer

An unmarked bottle
Not intended for refills
Screwed so tightly
I will never use it up

But twice a year, I let myself drink it in

>   The scent of money and coins and
>   sweat on henna-stained hands
>   The rush of half-second kisses and last-minute zakaat
>   The crackling of knees mixed with loudspeaker takbeers

>   And of course, the sight of your smile
>   Like the sugar syrup we poured
>   On microwaved gulab jamun

>   But was it heavy or light?
>   Crystal clear or blurred?
>   I don't think I can tell
>   The difference

>   I can't bring myself
>   To eat them that way
>   Anymore

All I want
                              Is you
            To always be

I don't use the perfume you wore to Eid prayer
It's an unmarked world I can't refill

I bottle these memories to keep them potent
So that twice a year, we say Eid Mubarak
In the drawer by my bed

The Ending Does Not Exist

Afeefah Khazi-Syed

when i was seven years old
my mother would take me to the nearby library
where i would pick out seven new books
for the seven days
ahead of me

i have emptied and filled bookshelves
young adult novels, physics textbooks, haitian ethnographies,
and everything in between

i never came across the perfect final chapter
left to search for solace
in midnight dreams

i cry when i leave a place
and i'm not very good at goodbyes
because when the essence of being
meets its fate
the sun rarely rises with a cry

will this be my last time

i have lost too many
to imperfect farewells and many a nights
it makes my head feel some kind of fuzzy

i try to remind myself

we were not built for endings
we were built to pull each other up
and pave our paths
to reunions of the afterlife

ON WOMEN

An Ode To The Things On My Face

Afeefah Khazi-Syed

they say that pimples are
a rite of passage
little protrusions of facial skin
that mark the entrance gate to
a place called adulthood

they come at a time
when life is tossed on its side
when innocent friendships outgrow and wither
when girl-turned-woman finally finds name
for that feeling of insecure

she has seen the world for all that it is:
imperfect   broken

and when she walks into the room
dressed in soft chiffon or flowing lawn
her subtle smile
is her pre-battle ritual

for facing an army of neighborhood aunties
equipped with newspaper columns
and group chat remedies

ice cube for ten minutes every night
rinse with rose water
pack with a miracle mixture of
rice flour egg white honey
moisturize with aloe vera pulp
munch on raw garlic
top with blots of sensodyne

oh meri jaan,
we must fix that face
discolorations must fade
make you
khoobsurat again
before it's too late

oh but aunty
if only you realized that the scars
will disappear
but the way you make me feel
hideous   insuffice
will always always persevere

stages of woman hood

Marwa Abdulhai

I. my father told me the best thing i could be
was his "behta"
strong, focused, studious, unfazed
"bindaas"
bangles and dresses stashed in the back of the closet
"only girls cry"
"will you be like your sister?"
constantly searching for validation in his eyes
"you are acting too much like a girl"

when i got my period
i didn't tell my mother for three days
until she found out
the shame was too much to bear
    "hide your pads"
    "don't go near the achaar"
    "where is your dupatta"
    "why are you speaking to that boy"

    "things will be different now"
another reminder
of my femininity.

i prayed to God every Ramadan
to make me look like anything but a woman
butt too big, the full chest, the hourglass
pilling fabric upon fabric
can i disappear?
these stares don't seem to stop

                    stop
            stop
stop.
"how about your daughter and my son?"
my mother said no, but what if she had not?

II. i saw girls back home get degrees
    as an entry fee for the marriage lottery
    our place was the home
    sacrifice is our family name
    there was no time for pursuit of choice

    then they came
    wanting to take back our narrative

    we had a narrative?
    for women and by women
    to reclaim our voices and our history
    unapologetically

    in the journey of putting pen to paper
    women i had never met became sisters
    brown and beautiful
    who had equal say in the household
    engineers, lawyers, homemakers, writers
    passionate, proud, pivotal, powerful
    all in one we uncovered stories of battles in spread of the message
                                                        Nusayba
    women who handled a business and saved an entire religion
                                                        Khadija
    we faced injustice in every era
    it never stopped
    but *things are different now.*

i feel pride in being a woman
the burden we bear has always been much greater
but it no longer scares me
we hustle, we dream, we fear and love
we are warriors despite it all

there is hair on my arms
i have stretch marks and desires
i now embrace them
dressing up perhaps a bit more
in celebration of this divine creation

III. I am a woman because
I had a special place in the heart of God.

Prayers You Whispered

Maisha M. Prome

You wore those saris until they softened like butter
Steamed in tarkari spices, simmered in summer
Dusted by loose earth when the courtyard was swept
Hand-scrubbed and line-dried before
the monsoon clouds wept
And when winter came, you sewed them together
Stitch by stitch with your still agile fingers
Those yards of well-worn cotton with their faded motifs
Into this blanket I hold tight around me as I sleep,
Wrapped in your love and the prayers you whispered,
Thousands of miles away.

In the Market for Mentors

Mariam Dogar

You're white
But not quite right
When you step into the room
And his eyes catch sight
Big desi nose and dark wild hair
Long silence as he stares
Three seconds and you're shook
When he puts down the book
That he authored in his prime

"Miriam,
Show me your student ID.
Tell me more about you
Before we talk biology."
But the questions that he asks
And the words that he says
Well they make you want to leave
And they leave you incensed

When you tell him about your job
And he asks about your dad
How he finds "this fine country!"
If Pakistan "is really that bad?"
When you mention your research
And he stops you in your tracks
He says that you're exotic
He asks more about your past

How your parents met
If your mom converted

Where you went to high school
He's shocked by Massachusetts
And then he loses interest
Picks up your student ID
"Such a nice photo of you here,
Don't you think?"

Is that okay?
He's almost seventy

But his name is on the walls
His prizes near his seat
And you almost forget
That you came here to learn
When he says his next words
About you being mixed race
And he says them with a grin
Spread wide around his face
Like he's proud of what he'll say

"You've got hybrid vigor!"
He proceeds to explain
And your mind goes green
And your mouth goes blank

Thanks?

"Like a species of corn,"
He helpfully adds
You grimace-smile back
And you tell yourself he meant
It as a compliment

Because what else do you do?
And who else do you have?

You've got four years left with him
And many like him after that
You know you're going to have to move
Through a far less settled path
Letting big things stick
And letting small ones pass
Before you can afford
To kick rocks at every a**

la regla

Ayse Guvenilir

8. make sure to not rezar namaz late.

9-20. it's normal life, i guess.

7. okay, today is finally gusül. how does that work, again?

21. i am starting to slip.

6. ha ha. no.

14. i lay on my back, resigned to feel the stabs.

22. why am i crying?

5. is it over?

23. i count.

4. oh, there it goes again, pounding.

24. oh, that's why i was crying. i always fall for it.

3. maybe i can live my life.

2. i have decided ibuprofen & dua are the only answers.

25. will the day arrive as scheduled? only sometimes.

1. why did i ever complain? and i sit on the toilet.

26. i kind of feel empty.

27. i guess i can try again, next time.

*28. why isn't it here?

ON HIATUS

it's not us

Mariam Dogar

we watched the sky fall together

the stars descended slowly
glittering warning signs and whispers
the moon's ending, instead, was abrupt
our last hug so swift it felt like a punch

now my home is
again, my casket
i'm tied to the ground
but far from grounded

a maddening meditation
because i know my cliffhanger
resides elsewhere
somewhere

at the intersection of my blank space

and yours

i feel this even as you push me away
i feel it every time i find a remnant of the sun

and when i start to move toward you again
the walls inside me tighten
they say: no promise is but a plan
a challenge to above
a gamble with ourselves

i pause
and i believe them

If Mutations Were Expected, Why Were We Caught Off Guard?

Afeefah Khazi-Syed

i am not strong enough
to relive
what happened after
they told me
you were dead

but in the few moments
that i let my eyes rest
i am hit with flashbacks
of walking into my mother's room
and realizing that you were really gone

i can feel something in the very depths of me
screaming to you

i think it is my soul

i did not know that souls were capable
of communicating like that

and when my eyes open again
each tear is a dulling of
a moment with you

> when i was little and you came to stay with us
> and you were napping and
> i sat on your tummy to wake you up

> the photo that i have of us at your graduation.
> you dressed in a black and green robe, me in my

marshmallow jacket

the pendant that you gave me for my graduation

you handed me your glasses at your wedding
—keep them safe, you said

you gave me three cousins
—you were supposed to be here to keep them safe

when my knee hit concrete, you immediately drove over
with my favorite Chinese takeout in hand

i would not have known of Taco Bell chalupas,
frozen yogurt, and Dunkin Donut hash browns without you

even in our last conversation,
you were teaching me how to build a website

why couldn't they wake you up from that ICU bed?

they are telling me to
have Sabr and Himmat and Thakkat

but it is easier to pretend that you have gone
on that cross country road trip
you said you would go on one day

January, 2021

Maisha M. Prome

It feels strange to be here
This time of year
The way the snow flurries down in coconut whirlwinds
How the geese never left for the southern warmth
The way the sky blazes the color of the river unfailingly
An ethereal frigidness,
      a petrified luminescence,
            a glass-painted quiescence
Lit by a sun whose reach falls unfelt on thick woolen coats
Yet its rays soothe, white-yellow like the edges of the pink flowers
That Spring will bring, to this place where even contentment aches
I have never seen winter like this before
I am usually home
This time of year

Submersion

Aleena Shabbir

The lull of the uncertainty
Is addicting in all ways
complacent comfort
Knowing that you control something
that cannot be controlled

I measure progress in waves
With each peak, comes a trove
When I'm happier I reverse it
Now, nothing but numbness

Filled to the brim with disquiet and despair
But not enough strength to confront
What is inside of me
All it takes is a few minutes of comfort, of compassion

Those things I won't give myself

I've been destroyed by my own perceptions
Relinquishing feels insurmountable

444 (no response)

Ayse Guvenilir

I haven't written a single word
typed a single letter
picked up a pen or pencil or marker
smelled the inside of a book
in what feels like ages.

I leave this room
pause from lying on this bed
for no more than one hour each day.

And it's not because my head feels cloudy
my throat keyed my nose packaged my body
screaming against infinite loops of dizzying movements
due to this random viral infection ravaging my body.

Pan   dem
   ic.

Grief in unnecessary self-imposed separation,
   that every attempt to process
      how I left all my friends behind, not knowing
         when I'll see any of them next. If I'll see them
           ever again—if Sars-CoV-2 and the injustices within
           society will even leave them the same

I
run
into
an

_ _ _ _ _.

ON BEING REAL

How Are You Doing?

Afeefah Khazi-Syed

i am finding it difficult to sleep at night

between hours of trying to
capture my existence into words
in hopes that someone else will see me

and the tears that i have tried crying but have yet to
over a life that no longer exists in my life

and the dread of not knowing when this
waiting period of mundanity will end

and the feeling of always needing to be
producing something
doing something
being something

all i want is
to be able to walk into a
cafe with my knapsack backpack in hand
surrounded by friends i can stand
feel my feet on land

i am lost
afraid of loose waterfalls
oceans that don't reach the shoreline
flowing rivers that never meet

i am not sure
i know
how i am

"Great! And you?"

No Lawyer Necessary

Aleena Shabbir

1. (a) "Practice what you preach"
      Words I always want to live by
   (b) Hypocrisy is scary
      So I have to make sure I try

2. (a) Be upfront and consistent
      Don't lie
   (b) No telling people what they want to hear
      A real ally

3. (a) Don't trash talk others
   (b) Or suddenly become shy

4. (a) Be authentic and live unapologetically
      But don't ever imply
   (b) Apathy or irresponsibility
      Irreparable reasons for goodbyes

5. (a) Love yourself and others
      Don't deny
   (b) Everyone is multifaceted
      Always apply
   (c) The benefit of the doubt to others
      All else beside

6. (a) Practice compassion and empathy
   (b) Show no judgment or surprise

7. (a) Cherish all your important ties
      You absolutely need the practice –
      One less regret when you die

Aleena Shabbir
_____
Self

I know you exist.
_____
Conscience

Off-key

Ayse Guvenilir

Maybe
       if you bleed enough tears
       you won't remember the silence
       the clanging of plates
       the sips of water
       the heavy breathing
       and oh, the silence.

it gets to you
louder than notes could be yelled
that diminuendo your soul
though you never quite know the tone

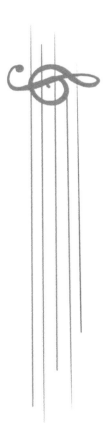

& maybe if you bleed enough tears
the chords will cadence

& these keys will just scar
for you to pick open
whenever chords disharmonize—
because they never stay harmonized.

coda or not you know
they will never resolve
but you say "it's nothing major"
it can't be.

if only you could bleed enough tears
you won't awaken tomorrow
with eyes somehow looking prettiest
accented in tears.

observation

Marwa Abdulhai

how much is enough
for me to believe?
just with my eyes that can see
the clouds moving in tandem with the trees
or tiny creatures surviving the coldest of seasons.
it's in the stars forming and colliding and collapsing
Insan created with language and will and feeling
a perfect design for life with probability of one in

100000000000000000000000000000000
000000000000000000000000000000000

you say everything serves a purpose
even the grains of sand placed along the sea
do they too feel Your presence?
stronger and closer to You than me?

i wonder at those previous
with patient fears and faith so resolute
could they tell me the secrets to the righteous path
we all seek?

Tangerine

Mariam Dogar

Lately I've been starting to feel my soul instead of my body
Like that day on the beach with the rocks and the sunset
Footsteps so faint I could almost levitate
With the horizon speaking into my ear: "Be content"

Or when I sat at the dinner table in the center of the forest
A citrus spread and the smell of durian between us
When he leaned forward and whispered
That he could feel his ancestors in the air

Or when I pass a tiger lily and feel a touch on my arm
Tracing the outline of the last day she could stand upright
When we walked in the garden and I painted her toes
A bright orange that decorated her feet on her deathbed

Or when my knees knock against a stranger's
And I remember us in the back of a sedan with a broken AC
Sharing secrets for hours in the delirious glow of the desert
Giving me inconvertible proof that you did exist

See I've come to the conclusion that I am not quite literal
I am memories transcribed without my knowledge
Like the passive rise and fall of my chest
Or the tears that slip from my eyes when I laugh

In this brilliant orchestra I collect these moments
Undeniably alive and imperfect and sentient
I am congruent with the hearts I've met before
And those He bids me to meet again

ON THE GROUND BENEATH ME

Live Thoughts As I'm Skydiving

Aleena Shabbir

I love the adrenaline
The thrill of adventure coursing inside

Scared out of my mind
I'm all over the place

Impulsive decisions are my strongest vice
Up until I'm actually out of my comfort zone

Arms flailing, deeply sinking
The wind whipping in my face

The lakes beneath me
Blue so beautifully different from the sky's

I never imagined I'd find it so ugly from here

"I hate this" while "I'm having the time of my life"
"Talk about a panorama" but "Did I just swallow a fly?!?"

Time seems more meaningful up here

I feel like I'm looking at a board game
Everything a tenth of its size

We get closer, the distance between us smaller,
but my fear, more real
What looked so tiny, now giant, daunting

I push my legs out, ready to come back and it's
The *"ass landing"* that grounds me again

And I'm thankful to the sky
I see things differently now

Rx for Sleep Paralysis

NAME: MARIAM DOGAR   DOB: XX / XX / XX

- frizzy carpet in your friend's dorm room
- cool hardwood of your cousin's house
- toasted sand in Wadi Rum
- your apartment's crackly couch
- hard cement floor in Lahore
- grass by your childhood porch
- sterile bench in an ICU
- patch of floor near the bed that you roll onto

ROUTE: TOPICAL   FREQUENCY: NIGHTLY

the most hearty sleep the patient has gotten
is from nights not spent in beds

sleep in sheets suffocates
she can't feel the ground
can't feel her spine
just feels her head

too often she is petrified
on the daily drift in and out of life
but laying in leftover places
fingers grazing wood & floor & earth

she escapes a mind
a body remembers how to work

in remembrance of the One

Marwa Abdulhai

half an hour before sunset
i rushed to make it just in time
for prayer in the masjid
Qur'an in one hand and a pillow in the other
during rest in runs of worship
long days of fasts and short nights of prayer didn't bother me
                         for prayer in the masjid
was of a different kind in this blessed month

nights pass as faces unknown become too familiar
the child who finds a chair for her mother
the mother who steps aside to cradle her crying child
in line for the same mercy on the same journey
to create meaning from this void
i wonder why i was chosen
to stand shoulder to shoulder with them in this very moment
                         for prayer in the masjid
was i a witness to the hopeful du'as, the patient du'as,
the desperate du'as
confessed on this night?
will these hands and feet and eyes be a witness
to my good and bad?
some thoughts linger longer when i raise my hands
          for prayer in the masjid

the angels said Ameen and Allah listened
as the cold morning came in
the world seemed just a little calmer
as i left and waited once more
for prayer in the masjid

Khatta Khanna

3 Cups of Rice
Cooking Oil
Mustard Seeds
Urad Dal
Channa Dal
Curry Leaves
Green Chillies
Hing
Salt
Haldi
4 Limes
Roasted Peanuts

Wash and cook 3 cups of rice and let cool. Heat half a tbsp of oil in pan for the tadka. Add mustard seeds, urad dal and channa dal. Saute until golden. Add curry leaves, freshly chopped green chillies. Let fry. Add hing, salt to taste. Add haldi for color. Squeeze juice from four limes and add to pan. Cook until simmering. Mix in cooked rice. Add in roasted peanuts and cover pan. Let sit until peanuts soften. Serve warm off the stove.

My Lunch Box: The Exotic Bazaar

Afeefah Khazi-Syed

i haven't even snapped open the blue lid
of my ikea tupperware when the blend of
spice and color meets your eye

a smile stretches across your face
as you pick up on the refined smell of Haldi and Garam Masala
staples of my mother's kitchen

but in reality there is a whiff in the air
different from the typical concoction of *PB&J*
MorningStar Nuggets and *Mac n' Cheese*

you hover over my seat at the long cafeteria table
calling my mother's Khatta Khanna
Neon Rice

the yellow carton of Frooti in my hand
is more tempting than
the *Apple Juice* or *Chocolate Milk* in yours

when i pull out my dessert
a ziploc bag of Kaju Katli,
you ask if i'm eating *silver*

"this is just for decoration"

the differences between our lunch boxes
is a difference of its own
it intrigues you
when you ask if you can try some
i smile back
ammi always knew to pack extras

A Thousand Places

Maisha M. Prome

Yellow earth between my toes,
    chasing chickens through the yard.
The slip on mosaic tile before
    the crash and the permanent scar.
A strip of airplane carpet
    miles above the gleaming sea.
Gritty greyness of the schoolyard
    scraping raw against my knee.

Polished floor of marbled tile
    like ice in the winter chill.
Dorm room carpet brown and warm
    with a history undistilled.
Treading through pearlescent snow
    and through monsoon-flooded streets,
I've walked a thousand places
    and found home beneath my feet.

Enough

Ayse Guvenilir

I have never been where
I will never go stuck
in this house with a heavy ceiling
reaching for the truth of what
I was trying to do
with you when I said
that I had to go
book the next flight out
would they ever trust me
a gringa—as Abuela dutifully reminds me—
otherwise?

Not that
given the current state of affairs
they would ever trust anyone
outside of whom could fix
every one of their problems bringing
them light
in the middle of the night
it's so hot
they can hear
their brain sweating feel
their sense slipping waiting
hours upon hours for gas shifts switching
in a car that is going to burn
anyways

the ground beneath my feet has never
felt more unstable than it feels right now
kids in CAGES the world AVOIDING
the humanitarian CRISIS—

                  like they avoid every crisis—
does anyone hear their cries into the echo
of the storage building
is it real? Does it matter?

How can I *be*
and *not* be saving
my home once-removed y
gente who I feel are my gente
bonded by lengua y risas y cultura
rooted in over exaggerations y bendiciones y
Dios te cuide y no te amo te adoro y
seemingly excessive abrazos y besos
that keep us whole.

Will I ever be enough
to save them all?

NOTES

ON MOTHERS

Parachute
This poem is named after Parachute hair oil—a staple to the many tel massages Afeefah grew up with.

A sampling of my favorite lullaby
The right aligned lines are lyrics from the popular lullaby, "Los Pollitos Dicen." The version seen in this poem was the one Ayse remembers hearing growing up, sung by her mother. "Los Pollitos Dicen," was originally a poem written by Chilean poet Ismael Parraguez and was first published in his 1907 book *Poesías Infantiles.*

I swear you were here
In grief and honor of Samar Dogar, Mariam's mother, who fought triple negative breast cancer and passed away Aug. 1st, 2018.

tranquility
فرشتے (Urdu) translates to angels.
inna lillahi wa inna ilayhi raji'un: transliteration of verse 2:156 of the Qur'an, translating to "to Allah we belong and to Him we shall return". This is said when you misplace something and would like to find it (as in the poem), as well as more frequently, when someone passes away.

ON SUMMER

when i think sunshine
This poem was written in the haibun form, a combination of a prose poem and a haiku.

ON LOVING

When in Dialogue

The line "if God willed, God would make them one community" is from the verse "Had Allah willed, He would have made you one nation [united in religion]" in the Qur'an (5:48).

"Aleena" isn't what I go by

All these words are in Urdu. Jaanu means sweetheart. Pyaari means pretty or cutie. Chalaak means smart in a clever, slightly cunning way. Meri zindagi means my life. Mera dil means my heart. Pagal means silly, nonsensical. Behta is an affectionate term for a child. Larki means girl.

ON THE UNSPOKEN

Hold Back

This poem was written after Ayse learned more about the experiences of Muslims during the war and genocide in Bosnia and Herzegovina from 1992 to 1995. A special thanks to Lejla for her care, thoughts, and consideration in the making of this poem.

i ask for Justice

"The Word" is used to denote the Holy Book of Muslims, the Qur'an. Meenambur is a village in the state of Tamil Nadu in South India.

Welcome Home

Jonmobhumi (Bengali) means country of birth.

ON MIGRATION

a citizenship

Haldi and zeera (Hindi/Urdu) translate to turmeric and cumin respectively. Jalfrezi is a chicken dish with a strong ginger and green chili flavor in South Asian cuisines. Sambaar is a dark brown, lentil stew common in South Indian cuisines. Abaya (Arabic) is a black dress worn by Muslim women. Hijab (Arabic) is a scarf worn by Muslim women to cover the head, neck, and chest and display modesty.

A Statement For The Confused

Contrary to what many expect, India is home to over 200 million Muslims. While the effects of the India-Pakistan partition of 1947 still echo through both nations, many Muslims in India live peacefully with their neighbors and friends and are just as Indian at the core. At the same time, Indian Muslims are not, as a whole, free of discriminatory institutions and politics.

ON HOME

The sun we haven't felt in years

This poem mentions the village where Mariam's father was born and raised in the Punjab province of Pakistan. -Wala or -Vala is a suffix used in Urdu, Hindi, and other languages and forms an adjectival compound of the noun it is attached to (i.e. Chaiwalla: the person serving chai). Arif was the name of a prominent farmer in the area with connections to the English government. When the English visited, they stayed with him. Later, upon elevating the village to a city, they named it after their friend. In 1908, the Deputy Governor of Punjab (English), "founded" the new city of Arifwala.

Alive

The last words of each line in the first stanza ("rooftop", "alive", and "desk") are taken and repeated in a different order in the remaining two stanzas. This is an example of a Tritina poem, a shorter version of the Sestina which contains six stanzas.

ON HOME AGAIN

Dear My Favorite Memories

320 is short for 20.320 Analysis of Biomolecular and Cellular Systems, a course required to complete the biological engineering undergraduate degree at MIT. The poem is a tribute to each person who recounted a memory to Ayse during a surprise Zoom call on her birthday.

the final destination

The river of our Prophet is in reference to the river Al-Kawthur granted to Prophet Muhammad upon the death of his son. It is found in Paradise, and is said to quench the thirst of all who arrive upon entry.

The Landing

Shezan is one of the best distributors in Pakistan for mango juice. Not completely biased in Aleena's opinion or anything. Absolutely not at all.

Dear Kashmir

In Fall 2019, just weeks after the Kashmiri lockdown went into effect, Afeefah attended a talk by Kashmiri filmmaker Musa Syeed. This poem was written shortly after as an ode to the people of Kashmir. The narrative, identity and rich culture of the Kashmiri people are often shadowed by the ongoing conflict between India, Pakistan, and China. Syeed's film *Valley of Saints* is a beautiful reclamation of the Kashmiri story.

ON FAITH

Sixth Grade

In 2011, the playground of Afeefah's local masjid—a place she and her family often visited—was burned to the ground in an act of arson. This is the first hate crime Afeefah consciously remembers experiencing. While her decision to wear hijab had nothing to do with this incident, Afeefah often looks back at the parallel narratives of her middle school years—a time in which she turned to hijab as an embracement of everything that she was. However, this was also a time in which Afeefah began to realize that not everyone in her community was accepting of who she was.

Empty

Allahu'akbar means God is great in Arabic. It is recited frequently in prayer and it is often used to express thankfulness to God. Unfortunately, the media has portrayed the term negatively, when in reality, it is used to express thankfulness to God, inside and outside of prayer.

Fleeting Faith

Halaqah (Arabic) is an informal or formal religious gathering within communities, where sermons or Islamic topics are discussed. Jumu'ah (Arabic) is the holiest day of the week, where special prayers are offered; usually around lunch hours. Khutbah (Arabic) is the weekly sermon that happens before every Jumu'ah prayer.

Submission

Allah is evoked by many names describing Allah's attributes. The translation of the Arabic word is placed on the bottom of each name of Allah in this poem. There are 99 names of Allah, and only a subset are mentioned.

Dadi

This poem is a prayer for Mariam's dadiummi (paternal grandmother). The poem references du'as, which are conversations a person has with God to share gratitude or hopes. Qur'an refers to the Muslim holy book. Insha'Allah means God-willing, usually expressing a humble promise or wish. Masha'Allah means God has willed it, usually expressing appreciation or joy. The poem also mentions a few foods Mariam only associates with her dadi, including halwa, a sweet dish made by frying semolina and saturating it with ghee and sugar, and tummy-ache sodas, which can be made with 1 Sprite can, 1 tbsp lemon juice, 1 tsp honey, and a little bit of love.

ON TONGUES

Rice
The poem references the Bangladesh Liberation War and the atrocities of the 1971 Bangladesh genocide committed by the Pakistani military. Many elders in Maisha's family fought in the war and her parents grew up in a nation rebuilding itself after independence. Decades earlier, the Bengal Famine of 1943 had killed more than 2 million people in the Bengal region (comprising present day Bangladesh and the Indian province of West Bengal). The famine arose not out of drought, but due to wartime policies imposed by the British colonial rule upon the region. (Sen, Amartya. *Poverty and Famines: An Essay on Entitlement and Deprivation.* Oxford: Oxford University Press, 1981)

zubaan
This poem was originally written in Urdu and translated into English. It references the following verse as translated by Yusuf Ali: "O mankind! We created you from a single (pair) of a male and a female, and made you into nations and tribes, that you may know each other…" in the Qur'an (49:13).

ON FORGETTING

i remember
Ayse's abuelo passed away in his home on January 12, 2019 in Barquisimeto, Venezuela.

Oud

Central to this poem are the feelings, imagery, and nostalgia surrounding Eid-al-Fitr – a celebration of the end of Ramadan, the month of fasting. It is one of the two large holidays in Islam. On Eid, Muslims traditionally dress in fancy or new clothes, congregate in masjids for prayer, wish each other "Eid Mubarak," give zakaat (charity), and eat food and desserts together. The Oud referenced in the poem is a fragrance that is warm, sweet, and woody and is used widely in the Arab world and elsewhere. Oud is usually very expensive, and is sold in small vials. Mariam's mother would save it for special events, such as Eid.

ON WOMEN

stages of woman hood

Behta is the Hindi/Urdu term to describe a male child. Achaar (Hindi/Urdu) is pickled vegetables/fruits cooked in spices and preserved in oil. In Marwa's culture there is a common superstition that going near certain foods when a woman is on her period will cause the foods to go bad.

Prayers You Whispered

Tarkari is another word for curry, usually one containing vegetables. It is a common part of South Asian cuisine.

In the Market for Mentors

Unfortunately, this was a real conversation Mariam had.

la regla

*First read through, start here; thereafter, start wherever.
The word regla (Spanish) is slang for menstruation. It also means: rule, ruler.

ON HIATUS

If Mutations Were Expected,
Why Were We Caught Off Guard?
The COVID-19 delta variant was first detected in India in October of 2020 and reached a peak in Spring 2021, killing over 400,000 individuals. Afeefah's mama (maternal uncle) was one of them. Hospitals were over capacity, oxygen tanks were hard to come by and the virus spread like wildfire through congested and crowded living quarters. Every single Indian family Afeefah knows has lost someone to the delta surge. This poem exists in this anthology as a remembrance of all the lives that were lost and all of the families that were left broken.

444 (no response)
What does _ _ _ _ _ mean? Hint: read into the title.

ON BEING REAL

observation
Insan (Arabic) translates to mankind.

ON THE GROUND BENEATH ME

in remembrance of the One
Ramadan is a blessed month for Muslims across the world, and is often spent at the masjid, a place of worship for Muslims. Muslims spend more of their time in prayer during the month, but also in du'a, a form of worship that seeks remembrance of or assistance from Allah. It can also be seen as a conversation a person has with Allah. Muslims also spend their time reading the Qur'an, the holy book of Islam. Muslims engage in this worship not only during Ramadan, but attempt to make it a part of their lives on a daily basis.

Enough

The two crises referenced are the immigration deportation and detainment along the border in the United States, and the continued political and economic hardships faced by many in Venezuela.

ACKNOWLEDGMENTS

It takes a lot of people to make a book come together, and our anthology, co-written by six poets, is no exception. We first would like to thank Layal and Hanna for being there at the start of it all, on that Friday night when we held our first poetry meeting in Room 707 of McCormick Hall. Many weekly meetings later, spanning almost three years, we now have this book. A special thanks to Hanna for penning our title and helping shape the beginnings of our anthology; it would not be published today as it is without you.

Thank you to Sara Bawany and others who helped edit this anthology. You helped us view our work from a critical lens, pushing our poems to be the best they could be. Thank you to Neghena, Mark Pawlak, and F.S. Yousaf for your valuable advice on the routes of publishing. Through the people we met along the way, we found our publisher, Beltway Editions. Thank you, Indran Amirthanayagam, for your encouragement from the very first time we met. You saw the potential in our work before we even had our first full draft and your support has been invaluable.

This anthology would not be complete without the beautiful artwork and designs that accompany it. Thank you to Zoe Norvell for creating our gorgeous cover. Thank you to Jorge Ureta Sandoval for the lovely book design. Thank you to Afeefah, one of our own poets, for creating the beautiful illustrations throughout the book. And thank you to both Afeefah and Mariam for the photographs provided in the anthology.

Growing up as children of immigrants in the US comes with many growing pains. But one advantage is that we are exposed to people from so many places, who we learn from and who learn from us. We have always deeply appreciated when people have taken the time to respectfully ask and learn about our cultural and faith backgrounds and to listen to our life experiences with compassion, especially if they were from a very different background. We want to thank each and every person who took the time to read our poems, and in doing so, carry forward the narratives we are sharing with the world.

Since the beginning of the project, we have valued incorporating multiple perspectives. Hence our poems are organized into On Somethings, showing a variety of approaches to the same prompt. We know that as writers, we are submerged in our own work, making us blind to the nuances of our poetry as experienced from external perspectives. We wanted to understand how our poems were perceived and understood in order to bring them to their best versions. Throughout the writing process, we hosted a series of "Focus Groups." We invited a number of people in our community—friends, cousins, classmates, professors, and mentors, all from different demographics and backgrounds—to come listen to our poetry. We read aloud chapters from earlier versions of our anthology and listened to their thoughts, reactions, and perceptions.

This feedback showed us how our creative choices translated and helped us see the shape of our intentions. Thank you to everyone who participated in our Focus Groups—Adina, Zaina, Memo, Alioune, Octavio, Samir, Maxine, Emily, Sara, Bryan, Harith, Abbas, Sally, Zaidi, Ayça, Zoha, Hala, Afreen, Safiya, Amina, Ezgi, Andrea M., Andrea O., Rumaisa, Numaan, Zuly, Shariqah, and everyone else who participated. Thank you to the many that have read our work beyond these Focus Groups as well. We are filled with gratitude for your company and conversation along the way.

We would also like to acknowledge the healthcare professionals and the vaccine research community for their tireless efforts to keep us safe and healthy throughout the pandemic. The vaccine inequity in the world has been atrocious, and it saddens us deeply. If you have the opportunity, please get vaccinated. If you can wear a mask to protect others (and yourself), please do. Thank you for taking care of each other throughout this pandemic.

This project began at MIT and stands as it is because of the many resources and connections we discovered there. Thank you to the Council of the Arts at MIT (CAMIT) and the MIT MindHandHeart grants for helping make this book possible. Thank you to the staff at MIT SOLE for facilitating this process. Moreover, thank you to Ed Barrett and Erica Funkhouser for providing feedback on our poems, both inside and outside of class, and supporting us in our publishing endeavors. And thank you to the MIT Muslim Students' Association (MSA) for not just your administrative and moral support throughout this project, but for fostering this beautiful community that we've called home since our very first days as undergrads.

This home of ours occupies "the traditional unceded territory of the Wampanoag Nation. We acknowledge the painful history of genocide and forced occupation of their territory, and we honor and respect the many diverse indigenous people connected to this land on which we gather from time immemorial. [Furthermore, we] acknowledge Indigenous Peoples as the traditional stewards of the land, and the enduring relationship that exists between them and their traditional territories." This is taken from the Land Acknowledgement Statement, developed by the MIT American Indian Science and Engineering Society (AISES) and the MIT Native American Student Association (NASA).

And thank you to our families. To our mothers and fathers. To brothers and sisters, grandparents, cousins, aunts, and uncles. To friends and roommates who have become family. To those who came before us all—our ancestors, our peoples. You inspired so much of our poetry, gave us the knowledge that we carry with us, and shaped so many of the memories we hold dearest in our hearts. Thank you for your sacrifices, for the love and lessons you've passed down without which we would not be here today.

We've grown so much since we started this project, and we could not have done it without the constructive criticism, celebration of unique skills, and support of one another. Our weekly meetings have been a grounding rod during a time when the world was in chaos. Reading each other's poetry and seeing it evolve has been a solace, an inspiration during difficult times. *Our Ancestors Did Not Breathe This Air* is more than just the poems. It is a coming together that brought us closer even as we finished college and started our individual journeys. We will share this for the rest of our lives, bridging ancestors and the many places we come from.

A heartfelt thanks to you, the reader, for taking this journey with us. We hope you will join us on our lifelong journeys to learn, grow, and appreciate through poetry.

Most of all, praise be to Allah, the most Gracious, the most Merciful. With You, we are guided. And without You, there would never have been poetry and most certainly not *Our Ancestors Did Not Breathe This Air.*

ABOUT THE POETS

Afeefah Khazi-Syed was born and raised in the DFW metroplex but has always called two places home: the suburbs of Texas and her grandparents' homes in Southern India. After studying biological engineering with a minor in urban studies at MIT, Afeefah finds herself on a new journey as a first-year medical student at UT Southwestern. She attributes her love for writing and storytelling to her grandparents' bedtime stories and the many writing mentors she has found throughout her life, from high school English teachers to other immigrant writers. Afeefah views poetry as a deeply personal exchange of experiences and stories.

Aleena Shabbir was born in Queens, New York and has lived in New York ever since. As a Pakistani-US-American, she cherishes connecting with a multitude of cultures, in addition to her own roots. Many years after the minor poetry lessons she had taken in elementary school, Aleena found a community with these fellow poets who have taught her how to express herself creatively and comfortably; she is forever grateful for them and their care. Having studied data science/operations research and different fields of applied mathematics, Aleena hopes to one day work in policy development with a quantitative background. Aleena usually enjoys reading, anything to do with nature, traveling, and pursuing adrenaline inducing experiences.

Ayse Angela Guvenilir was born in Austin into a family with a Turkish father, a Venezuelan mother, and three older brothers. Growing up in Texas, France, and various parts of upstate New York, Ayse has always used reading and writing for connection, reflection, and relaxation as she moved from place to place. She sees poetry in particular as a form of writing that can surpass the bounds of what words are expected to be, in turn connecting her with others. Ayse got her bachelor's degree in biological engineering with a minor in creative writing from MIT and is currently a master's student in the Biomechatronics Group at the MIT Media Lab. Through her work, Ayse aims to empathize, educate, and inspire, the way that the works of others have always done for her.

Maisha Munawwara Prome was born in Dhaka, Bangladesh and has moved back and forth between Bangladesh and the United States throughout her life. Maisha used to write poetry as a child growing up in New York City, but rediscovered it in college while taking classes for her writing minor. Aside from poetry, Maisha enjoys all things creative, from baking to crocheting to writing fiction. She has won awards for her short stories and hopes to continue writing alongside working in research and education. Maisha graduated from MIT with a bachelor's degree in biological engineering. She is currently pursuing her Ph.D. in biological sciences at Yale University.